RECONCILIATION

Restoring Broken Relationships

JUNE HUNT

AspirePress

Torrance, California

Reconciliation: Restoring Broken Relationships
Copyright © 2014 Hope For The Heart
All rights reserved.
Aspire Press, a division of Rose Publishing, Inc.
4733 Torrance Blvd., #259
Torrance, California 90503 USA
www.aspirepress.com

Printed in the United States of America
010114DP

CONTENTS

ear friend,

Personally, I know what it's like to feel the pain of a broken relationship—I mean, the hurt, the heartache of a ruined relationship. What agony!

And I know what it's like to yearn and pray for a restored relationship—a heart-to-heart reconciliation, only to have that reconciliation clearly denied. No matter how much I tried or how much I prayed, the relationship was never restored. And it took years for my heart to heal.

However, I also know what it's like to have a reconciled relationship—with wrongs fully forgiven and hurts wholly healed. The pain of the past remains completely in the past. What peace, what ease, what joy—this is ultimate freedom! I consider this reconciled relationship a gift from God—a gift of grace from God.

But this kind of reconciliation doesn't "just happen." It requires a commitment of both *quality time* and *quantity time* to the relationship. This kind of focused attention involves processing pain from the past, forgiving what was fracturing, and rebuilding a new relationship based on renewed trust.

If a reconciled relationship is the desire of

your heart, my sincere prayer is that you will find the path to freedom within these pages. Remember, however, even if you have a heart for reconciliation, *it takes two to reconcile a relationship*. You can't force it, but you can pave the way for it.

As you do all you can do, rest in your relationship with the Lord—you can find your peace in Him.

With shared compassion,

June

June Hunt

May these words be meaningful to you, as they have been to me: *"If it is possible, as far as it depends on you, live at peace with everyone"* (Romans 12:18).

RECONCILIATION
Restoring Broken Relationships

In a broken world, things break, including relationships. Miscommunication, misbehavior, and misinformation can unravel the tightest bonds and leave emotions spinning out of control. Everyone experiences relationship breakdowns because imperfect people are connected to other imperfect people. But the Bible makes it clear that our hearts should be a reflection of God's heart, which ultimately is a heart of reconciliation.

Romans 5:8 tells us, *"God demonstrates his own love for us in this: While we were still sinners, Christ died for us."* Notice how we—the offending party who have sinned—didn't have to apologize first or get cleaned up first in order for God to make a move. Instead, He reached out in sacrificial love, longing for us to be reconciled to Him, longing for us to have a relationship with Him.

In the end, when we learn how to reconcile. We learn how to reflect God's character.

"God was pleased to have all his fullness dwell in him, and through him to reconcile to himself all things, whether things on earth or things in heaven, by making peace through his blood, shed on the cross." (Colossians 1:19–20)

DEFINITIONS

Nick is stuck—seemingly chained to his dead-end work with no opportunity for advancement. The environment is stifling and the work mundane, the same day in and day out as he languishes in deepening despair. Nick looks around at his coworkers, their long, tired faces signaling that they have given up on their hopes and dreams. They know they will never aspire to anything more than this.

The man over him sounds the stern command: "Get back to work!" Nick jolts back to the task at hand. Not much time to muse in these surroundings; just work, work, work.

Then, one day Nick realizes he's had enough. He has to break free from this belittling bondage, so he comes up with a plan.

Yet the Bible tells us that God is ultimately in charge of every plan.

> **"In his heart a man plans his course,**
> **but the LORD determines his steps."**
> **(Proverbs 16:9)**

Broken relationships began in the Garden of Eden when Adam and Eve sinned and disrupted the intimate fellowship they had with God. The need for reconciliation between God and each of us has existed ever since sin entered the world and was passed from one generation to the next! At one time we were enemies of God, going our own way apart from Him, but Christ made it possible for us to be reconciled to God.

The Bible offers this encouragement:

"For if, when we were God's enemies,
we were reconciled to him through the
death of his Son, how much more,
having been reconciled,
shall we be saved through his life!"
(Romans 5:10)

When the opportune time comes, Nick escapes. Nick runs.

He feels he has to get away, far away, from the suffocating atmosphere that continually squelches his personal growth and self-esteem. Nick travels over land and sea to the big city, seeking to immerse himself in countless opportunities to start over. In regard to his former work, he recognizes that reconciliation with Phil, the owner, will now be impossible since he quit and disappeared. No matter what, he must make things work in the city.

So many sights and sounds, so many faces and fears. But then Nick's ears are drawn to a voice on a city street, boldly proclaiming something about the Good News, something about the gospel of Christ, someone proclaiming the greatest story ever told—the basic message being ...

> **"I want you to know that through Jesus the forgiveness of sins is proclaimed to you."**
> **(Acts 13:38)**

▶ **Reconciliation** is the act of settling or harmonizing differences, especially resolving differences between one another. While a relationship will not always be salvaged, the spirit of reconciliation always reflects the heart of God.

▶ **Reconciliation** between God and human beings is based on:

#1 Atonement, a sacrificial act that covers a person's sins and brings that person into reconciliation with God

- The Hebrew word *kaphar* means "to cover," which is most often translated as atonement.[1]

"Through love and faithfulness sin is atoned for" (Proverbs 16:6).

#2 Jesus Christ, who became the sacrifice for our sins

- The Greek word *katallasso*, means "to change or exchange."[2] He settled our debt, reconciling us to God and giving us a ministry of reconciliation to others. The Bible confirms this truth:

"All this is from God, who reconciled us to himself through Christ and gave us the ministry of reconciliation."
(2 Corinthians 5:18)

> I OWED A DEBT I COULD NOT PAY.
> HE PAID A DEBT HE DID NOT OWE.[3]

▶ Types of reconciliation[4]

- *Relational*: to bring a broken relationship into harmony
- *Personal*: to be at peace with our circumstances or with ourselves
- *Financial*: to bring accounting records into agreement
- *Spiritual*: to be at harmony with God

BIBLICAL EXAMPLE OF RECONCILIATION

Joseph (Genesis 37:2–45:15)

The Bible is a relational textbook. The Old Testament story of Joseph is one of family conflict—full of jealousy, bitterness, and betrayal. Surrounded by older brothers who hate him, Joseph is treated unmercifully, sold into slavery, and destined to live in a pagan country under extreme pressure. Few of us escape the pain of a loved one's rejection. The all-too-easy response is to cling to the offense and, in doing so, reject the heart of forgiveness.

Even in the face of false accusation, Joseph does not lose his faith. Over time he is promoted from a prison to a palace and becomes second in power to Pharaoh. Ultimately, God orchestrates events in Joseph's life to bring about a showdown with his brothers. He must now choose between hardening his heart or reflecting God's heart. With immense compassion, Joseph forgives his brothers and initiates the ministry of reconciliation. (See Genesis 37–50.) The Bible describes this tender moment:

> **"And he kissed all his brothers
> and wept over them.
> Afterward his brothers talked with him."
> (Genesis 45:15)**

If anyone needs Good News, it's Nick.

He is alienated from all he's ever known—totally alone. Yet he encounters a man who talks about the great love of God and the great sacrifice of God: sending His Son, Jesus, who died on the cross for all of our sins and then rose from the dead three days later. Nick learns that he can have his sins forgiven and that he will go to heaven, but he also discovers that God wants to be involved in his life right now, guiding him and helping him. Nick cannot seem to resist such irresistible love, so his new friend, Raul, leads him into a relationship with Jesus. They immediately form a close bond as brothers in Christ. Raul is the embodiment of this verse:

> **"A friend loves at all times,**
> **and a brother is born for adversity."**
> **(Proverbs 17:17)**

▶ **Alienation** occurs when a person withdraws or separates from another person, causing one to be excluded from others.[5]

- The Hebrew word *rāchaq* means to "be or become far, distant" or to be "removed." The word normally applies to great distances but can also apply to alienation between individuals.[6] The Hebrew word *zur* most often refers to "a stranger" but is sometimes translated "estranged."[7]

"He has alienated my brothers from me; my acquaintances are completely estranged from me" (Job 19:13).

- **Alienation** in Greek is *apallotriō*, which means "to estrange," that is, "to be shut out from one's fellowship and intimacy."[8] The word is translated "exclude," "separate," or "alienate."

"Once you were alienated from God and were enemies in your minds because of your evil behavior. But now he has reconciled you by Christ's physical body through death to present you holy in his sight, without blemish and free from accusation" (Colossians 1:21–22).

▶ **Types of alienation**[9]

- *Relational*: unfriendliness or hostility toward friends, family, or the values of others
- *Personal*: withdrawal from people, difficulty in developing relationships with others
- *Legal*: alienation of affections (marriages ending in divorce)—the conveyance or transfer of property to another
- *Spiritual*: separation from God because of sin

BIBLICAL EXAMPLE OF ALIENATION

David (2 Samuel 13:1–18:33)

Many parents feel the pain and remorse of knowing that they have failed. David's personal relationship with his son Absalom is one of the most heartrending examples of anger, bitterness, and unforgiveness among close family members. David's son Amnon rapes his own half sister, Tamar. When David fails to punish Amnon, Tamar's full brother Absalom takes matters into his own hands and kills Amnon. David's detachment from his children sets up such agonizing alienation that events deteriorate from family discord to physical death. Ultimately, Absalom rebels against both David and God and meets a violent death. Scripture reveals King David's pain.

> "The king was shaken.
> He went up to the room over the gateway
> and wept. As he went, he said:
> 'O my son Absalom!
> My son, my son Absalom!
> If only I had died instead of you—
> O Absalom, my son, my son!'"
> (2 Samuel 18:33)

Rewind about 2,000 years ago to the original cast of biblical characters.

"Nick" is actually Onesimus, the runaway slave of "Phil," who is Philemon. "Raul" is the apostle Paul, who speaks truth and hope into Onesimus' life like he speaks truth and hope into downtrodden lives today through Scripture. Onesimus is representative of so many people around the world, enslaved to hopelessness, fear, alienation, and despair. But the Good News, the Gospel of Jesus Christ, transforms Onesimus' life as it continues to transform countless other lives.

Onesimus tells Paul everything about his former life—his work environment and his running away. Subsequently, Paul takes on another role in addition to friend and mentor—*that of mediator*. Onesimus must address several major issues, but he cannot do this by himself. Scripture implies that he stole money from Philemon for his long journey to Rome, so Paul mediates to make sure the matter is settled. In a poignant illustration of our sin being charged to Christ—fully placed onto Christ on the cross—Paul tells Philemon to charge Onesimus' debt to his account. In Paul's own words: *"If he has done you any wrong or owes you anything, charge it to me. I, Paul, am writing this with my own hand. I will pay it back"* (Philemon 18–19).

BIBLICAL EXAMPLE OF MEDIATION

Abigail (1 Samuel 25:2–42)

Abigail's ministry of mediation surfaces in the story of two men in great conflict, David and her surly husband, Nabal. A wealthy landowner, Nabal refuses David's legitimate request for food and shelter by hurling insults at him and his ragged army. Wisely assuming the role of mediator between these two highly angered men, Abigail staves off David's impending revenge by first serving him and his men a meal fit for kings. She then appeals to David's sense of godly leadership, and he ultimately praises her for her good judgment. Abigail is a fine example of an effective mediator—her persuasive arguments and actions portray wisdom that leads to conflict resolution.

> "Then David accepted from her hand what she had brought him and said, 'Go home in peace. I have heard your words and granted your request.'"
> (1 Samuel 25:35)

With obedience comes blessing, and it is God's heart to bring peace where there is pain, to bring freedom where there is emotional bondage. A slew of negative emotions surround rejecting hearts, those who refuse to try to restore broken relationships. But for those who are obedient to the call of Scripture—to reach out in Christlike love toward reconciliation—even the most broken of relationships can be healed. The very real truth is this: *With God, there is no relationship that cannot be restored.*

Heed this admonition from Scripture:

> **"Make every effort to be found spotless, blameless and at peace with him."**
> **(2 Peter 3:14)**

▶ **Rejecting** relationships leads to disunity and dysfunction.

Restoring relationships lets healing and harmony prevail.

Romans 12:16 says, *"Live in harmony with one another. Do not be proud."*

▶ **Rejecting** relationships grieves the heart of God.

Restoring relationships gladdens the heart of God.

Philippians 2:2 says, *"Make my joy complete by being like-minded, having the same love, being one in spirit and purpose."*

▶ **Rejecting** relationships signals unforgiveness.

Restoring relationships signifies forgiveness.

Luke 6:37 says, *"Forgive, and you will be forgiven."*

▶ **Rejecting** relationships deepens guilt and drains joy.

Restoring relationships dissipates burdensome emotions.

Psalm 38:4 says, *"My guilt has overwhelmed me like a burden too heavy to bear."*

▶ **Rejecting** relationships breeds deep-seated anger and hostility.

Restoring relationships brings about peace.

Ephesians 4:26 says, *"'In your anger do not sin': Do not let the sun go down while you are still angry."*

▶ **Rejecting** relationships misses opportunities to show mercy.

Restoring relationships mirrors the character of God.

Psalm 25:6 says, *"Remember, O Lord, your great mercy and love, for they are from of old."*

CHARACTERISTICS

No one escapes the pain of relationships that are in conflict. Relatives refuse to speak for years because of a dispute at the Thanksgiving Day dinner table. Courtrooms are brimming with litigation between coworkers, neighbors, and angry spouses. Even churches can't escape the destruction of discord.

Examine your own heart. Do you hold on to attitudes that alienate, or do you reflect God's heart—a heart of reconciliation, a heart of peace?

Jesus describes those who endeavor to make peace.

> **"Blessed are the peacemakers,
> for they will be called sons of God."
> (Matthew 5:9)**

Deserted. It's a word that the apostle Paul associates with John Mark. This deserter, along with his cousin Barnabas, had been traveling and ministering with Paul. The three had been on their first missionary journey, with John Mark's designated role as "helper" to the other two. Paul and Barnabas were proclaiming the gospel and planting churches throughout Asia Minor, but halfway through the journey, John Mark "bails" and returns to Jerusalem. Together with Barnabas, Paul continues to carry the Good News of Jesus.

> "We tell you the good news:
> What God promised our fathers
> he has fulfilled for us,
> their children, by raising up Jesus."
> (Acts 13:32–33)

But not all who hear the Good News have receptive hearts. The Bible warns about those who alienate rather than align with God's will:

> "For I see that you are full of bitterness
> and captive to sin."
> (Acts 8:23)

Consider the characteristics of an alienating heart:[17]

▶ **Pride**: Do I focus only on the personal injustice of how much I've been wronged?

▶ **Faultfinding**: Do I dwell on the mistakes of others and fail to recognize my own faults?

▶ **Resentment**: Do I hold on to my anger until it develops into bitterness?

▶ **Avoidance**: Do I avoid being around the person with whom I have conflict?

▶ **Silence**: Do I close the door on communication by refusing to share my feelings in a healthy way?

▶ **Isolation**: Do I detach and withdraw from the person physically or emotionally?

▶ **Unfaithfulness**: Do I share unnecessary information with others and act in an untrustworthy manner?

▶ **Hopelessness**: Do I lack the faith that God can work in any situation?

"See to it that no one misses the grace of God and that no bitter root grows up to cause trouble and defile many."
(Hebrews 12:15)

Clearly Paul doesn't consider the exit justifiable when talk of a second missionary journey begins to stir. Barnabas wants to take John Mark with them again, *"but Paul did not think it wise to take him, because he had deserted them ... and had not continued with them in the work"* (Acts 15:38). Neither is able to persuade the other. They have *"such a sharp disagreement"* (Acts 15:39) that they end up parting ways.

Ultimately, Barnabas takes John Mark and sails eastward for Cyprus, while Paul chooses Silas and travels northward through provinces in Asia Minor in order to strengthen the existing churches.

The two teams are anything but united, even though the Bible says ...

"Make my joy complete by being like-minded, having the same love, being one in spirit and purpose."
(Philippians 2:2)

Consider the characteristics of those with a heart of reconciliation:

▶ **Humility:**[18] Do I focus on how much the Lord continues to forgive me?

▶ **Self-examination:**[19] Do I expect change only in others, or do I recognize my own need to change also?

▶ **Forgiveness:**[20] Do I choose to release my personal rights and allow the Lord to empower me to forgive?

▶ **Confrontation:**[21] Do I communicate my feelings without accusation?

▶ **Communication:** Do I set aside quality time to share my heart and have personal interaction?

▶ **Risk taking:** Do I risk rejection, knowing that God's love and acceptance will fulfill me?

▶ **Commitment:** Do I set aside my personal hurt for the sake of the relationship?

▶ **Confidence:** Do I trust God to heal my heartaches and to meet my needs?

> **"The one who calls you is faithful
> and he will do it."
> (1 Thessalonians 5:24)**

Broken relationships. What kind of heart will the men of God manifest? Hearts that alienate or hearts that seek reconciliation?

As a testimony to their obedience to God, all three men—Barnabas, John Mark, and Paul—reconcile with one another, and their ministry partnership continues. In fact, when Paul is imprisoned in Rome, anticipating his death and writing his final letter (2 Timothy), he rallies his friends to his side, and John Mark is a noted member of the group.

Paul's directive in 2 Timothy 4:11 states, *"Get Mark and bring him with you, because he is helpful to me in my ministry."* This illustrates the power of making peace when hearts are aligned with the Prince of Peace, Jesus.

> **"I appeal to you, brothers, in the name of our Lord Jesus Christ, that all of you agree with one another so that there may be no divisions among you and that you may be perfectly united in mind and thought."**
> **(1 Corinthians 1:10)**

A mediator seeks to:

▶ **Promote unconditional acceptance** between those who are estranged

▶ **Encourage mutual forgiveness** between alienated parties

▶ **Establish fair, clear, honest, and loving communication** between those with unresolved issues

▶ **Reveal personal value** and worth of individuals who are in opposition to one another

▶ **Gain and share insights** into underlying, unmet needs of both people involved

▶ **Explore avenues** of reestablishing trust between conflicted parties

▶ **Discover common ground** for agreement and reconnection between previous cohorts

▶ **Revitalize positive relationships** by focusing on past meaningful experiences shared by loving friends who are at odds with one another

God's Word encourages expressions of love and peace between all who belong to the body of Christ:

> **"Greet one another with a kiss of love. Peace to all of you who are in Christ."**
> **(1 Peter 5:14)**

Reconciliation vs. Forgiveness

QUESTION: "Is reconciliation the same as forgiveness?"

ANSWER: No, reconciliation and forgiveness are not the same because ...

▶**Reconciliation** focuses on the relationship.

  Forgiveness focuses on the offense.

▶**Reconciliation** requires at least two people.

  Forgiveness requires only one person.

▶**Reconciliation** is necessarily reciprocal, directed two-ways.

  Forgiveness is not necessarily reciprocal, but can be directed only one-way.

▶**Reconciliation** is the choice to rejoin the offender.

  Forgiveness is the choice to release the offender.

▶**Reconciliation** involves a change in behavior by the offender.

  Forgiveness involves a change in thinking about the offender.

▶**Reconciliation** is a restored relationship based on restored trust.

Forgiveness is a free gift to the one who has broken trust.

▶**Reconciliation** is offered to the offender because it has been earned.

Forgiveness is extended even if it is never, ever earned.

▶**Reconciliation** is conditional, based on repentance.

Forgiveness is unconditional, regardless of a lack of repentance.

▶**Reconciliation** necessitates an agreed upon relationship.

Forgiveness necessitates no relationship at all.

The Bible asks this rhetorical question:

> **"Do two walk together**
> **unless they have agreed to do so?"**
> **(Amos 3:3)**

Reconciliation after Forgiveness

QUESTION: "After we forgive someone, does God always expect us to be reconciled to that person?"

ANSWER: The answer to this question is both *yes* and *no*.

▶ Most of the time, God desires that we be reconciled to one another.

Second Corinthians 5:18 says, *"God ... reconciled us to himself through Christ and gave us the ministry of reconciliation."*

▶ At other times God considers the restoration of a relationship to be unwise, as in the case of adulterous partners or unrepentant abusers and their victims.

First Corinthians 15:33 says, *"Do not be misled: 'Bad company corrupts good character.'"*

▶ Likewise, if a husband exhibits a violent temper, his wife needs to move out of harm's way until he has received counseling that has led to permanent, positive changes in his lifestyle.

Proverbs 22:24 says, *"Do not make friends with a hot-tempered man, do not associate with one easily angered."*

▶ Additionally, there are instances when a former relationship was unhealthy due to being unbalanced, codependent, or dishonoring to God in other ways. In such cases, the two people may be reconciled to one another but their relationship would necessarily need to change and take on healthy attributes.

As Ephesians 4:22–24 says, "*You were taught, with regard to your former way of life, to put off your old self, which is being corrupted by its deceitful desires; to be made new in the attitude of your minds; and to put on the new self, created to be like God in true righteousness and holiness.*"

▶ Reconciliation does not mean the relationship that previously existed between two people will necessarily be the same as it was before there was a break in the relationship. People and relationships are fluid and always changing, either by design or by default.

According to Proverbs 27:17, we are to seek to help one another change by design, "*As iron sharpens iron, so one man sharpens another.*"

▶ Relationships that have the best prognosis for survival and improvement over time are those in which the participants consciously make choices to make the relationship better and to keep it from becoming static and rigid. The same is true in our relationship with God, who always faithfully works in our lives to transform us into His likeness while we faithfully work to cooperate with Him.

"And we, who with unveiled faces
all reflect the Lord's glory,
are being transformed into his likeness
with ever-increasing glory,
which comes from the Lord,
who is the Spirit."
(2 Corinthians 3:18)

CAUSES OF IRRECONCILABLE DIFFERENCES

It is a broken relationship that begins in the womb. During Rebekah's pregnancy her twin babies continually jostle with each other, foreshadowing future tumult and turmoil. Rebekah inquires of the Lord, and He responds: *"Two nations are in your womb, and two peoples from within you will be separated; one people will be stronger than the other, and the older will serve the younger"* (Genesis 25:23).

The first to be born is a boy described as reddish, *"and his whole body was like a hairy garment"* (Genesis 25:25). He is called Esau because "hairy" is a Hebrew pun on the name. Next comes another boy, grasping his brother's heel. He is named Jacob, which means "heel catcher" and "trickster." Both names, it will turn out, couldn't be more appropriate.

As the boys grow up, they are opposites in every way, which will contribute to years of irreconcilable differences. But the primary reason for their broken relationship concerns the coveted birthright of the firstborn.

Scripture wisely discerns ...

**"What causes fights and quarrels among you? Don't they come from your desires that battle within you?
You want something but don't get it.
You kill and covet, but you cannot have what you want.
You quarrel and fight."
(James 4:1–2)**

"Irreconcilable differences," a legal term, is recognized in many countries as grounds for divorce. This simple courtroom plea breaks the bonds of holy matrimony, minimizing the fault of either party. The cause of the divorce is not attributed to one specific act of misconduct or improper behavior. Thus the "broad-brush" ruling provides a convenient way for diminishing any personal blame for the breakdown of the marriage relationship. Unfortunately, attitudes that are behind these laws contribute to the moral decline of any culture because God created marriage to be a lifetime commitment. We are ultimately accountable for how we interact with others. A hardened heart that refuses to take responsibility in life only invites trouble in life.

**"Blessed is the man who always fears the Lord, but he who hardens his heart falls into trouble."
(Proverbs 28:14)**

"Quick, let me have some of that red stew! I'm famished!" (Genesis 25:30).

Esau, a skilled hunter, has just returned home from the open field, and the aroma of Jacob's bubbling red stew heightens his hunger to the breaking point. Jacob—cool and calculating—perceives an opportune moment concerning his brash brother and makes a proposal: *"First sell me your birthright"* (Genesis 25:31). Jacob's increasingly hardened heart is ready to "seal the deal."

The holder of the birthright becomes the predominant son and is promised a double share of his father's inheritance. But Esau is solely focused on his hunger pangs and foolishly replies, *"Look, I am about to die ... What good is the birthright to me?"* (Genesis 25:32). So the exchange is made and the day soon comes when Esau and Jacob's aging and blind father, Isaac, will bestow the birthright blessing.

Eager to bestow the blessing upon his eldest son, Isaac tells Esau to go catch and prepare some wild game for him to eat first. Rebekah overhears the instruction, and while Esau is away she covers the neck and hands of her favorite son, Jacob, with goatskins and clothes him in

Esau's finest garb. This scheming twin now feels and smells like his "hairy" brother, and Jacob fools his father into bestowing the priceless birthright blessing upon him instead. In Isaac's words: *"May God give you of heaven's dew and of earth's richness—an abundance of grain and new wine. May nations serve you and peoples bow down to you. Be lord over your brothers, and may the sons of your mother bow down to you"* (Genesis 27:28–29).

Someone with a hardened heart:

▶ **Dislikes** confrontation

▶ **Denies** that conflict exists

▶ **Dwells** on personal injustice received

▶ **Dominates** conversation and makes no concessions

▶ **Demonstrates** pride

▶ **Deceives** others about personal feelings

▶ **Discusses** the problem with defiance

▶ **Distrusts** the motives of others

▶ **Defends** personal views

▶ **Deafens** ears to apologies

▶ **Deflates** any solutions offered

▶ **Develops** apathy

▶ **Detaches** emotionally

▶ **Determines** not to be hurt again

▶ **Disapproves** of seeking a mediator

▶ **Deduces** that the other person will never change

▶ **Desires** revenge

▶ **Damages** the reputation of the other person

▶ **Disowns** personal responsibility

▶ **Discounts** past commitments

**"A man who remains stiff-necked
after many rebukes will suddenly be
destroyed—without remedy."
(Proverbs 29:1)**

We have all been created with three God-given inner needs: the needs for love, significance, and security.[22]

▶ **Love**—to know that someone is unconditionally committed to our best interest

"My command is this: Love each other as I have loved you" (John 15:12).

▶ **Significance**—to know that our lives have meaning and purpose

"I cry out to God Most High, to God, who fulfills his purpose for me" (Psalm 57:2).

▶ **Security**—to feel a sense of belonging and acceptance

"He who fears the LORD has a secure fortress ..." (Proverbs 14:26).

At the core of our own negative behavior is an attempt to get our legitimate needs met in illegitimate ways—the Bible calls this sin.

> **"There is a way that seems right ...
> but in the end it leads to death."
> (Proverbs 14:12)**

Why did God give us these deep inner needs, knowing that "people fail people"? (We all know of people who can be harsh, cruel, and abusive.)

While everyone has been created with three God-given inner needs, no single person is capable of meeting all of those needs. Realize, if one person could meet all of our needs, then we wouldn't need God!

By God's design, Jesus Christ is intended to be the Need-Meeter for every person who has ever lived.

The apostle Paul revealed this truth by exclaiming, *"What a wretched man I am! Who will rescue me from this body of death?"*

Then he answered his own question in the most definitive way: *"Jesus Christ our Lord!"* (Romans 7:24–25).

All along, the Lord planned to meet our deepest needs for ...

▶ **Love**: *"I [the Lord] have loved you with an everlasting love; I have drawn you with loving-kindness"* (Jeremiah 31:3).

▶ **Significance**: *"'I know the plans I have for you,' declares the LORD, 'plans to prosper you and not to harm you, plans to give you hope and a future'"* (Jeremiah 29:11).

▶ **Security**: *"The LORD himself goes before you and will be with you; he will never leave you nor forsake you. Do not be afraid; do not be discouraged"* (Deuteronomy 31:8).

The Lord will meet certain needs by Himself, and at other times He will use others as an extension of His care and compassion.

The Bible gives this assurance:

> **"My God will meet all your needs according to his glorious riches in Christ Jesus." (Philippians 4:19)**

People who struggle with reconciliation can have a false sense of significance, namely pride, that keeps them from reaching out to their offenders. They can't bear the idea of humbling themselves in order to make the first move toward relationship restoration; therefore, pride prevails and brokenness continues. A legitimate need for significance exists, but it is being met in an illegitimate way.

The need for security prevents some people from reconciling, and their fears of being hurt again keep their broken relationships forever broken. All fear should be replaced with faith, trusting God with the outcome as obedient steps toward reconciliation are taken.

Both parties in a broken relationship need to realize that they each have these three God-given needs. For those who have been offended, your offenders need to be loved, even if they don't show it on the outside. It is God's sovereign design encompassing all ages, races, genders, and socioeconomic groups.

We are called to love, and we are called to be seekers of reconciliation. In Proverbs, often called the book of wisdom, we are directed ...

> **"If your enemy is hungry,**
> **give him food to eat;**
> **if he is thirsty, give him water to drink.**
> **In doing this, you will heap**
> **burning coals on his head,**
> **and the Lord will reward you."**
> **(Proverbs 25:21–22)**

For example, helping out a neighbor in need is like giving food and drink to the hungry and thirsty. The "burning coals" of kindness could be the very thing that brings about godly sorrow that in turn may lead to repentance and reconciliation.

Seeking reconciliation is stepping out in obedience and, according to this proverb, it is something that will be rewarded.

> **"He who scorns instruction**
> **will pay for it, but he who respects**
> **a command is rewarded."**
> **(Proverbs 13:13)**

Exit Jacob. Enter Esau.

No sooner has Jacob left his father's presence when Esau returns, eager to receive a lifetime of blessing. When they both realize the "schemer" has deceived them, Esau bursts out with a bitter cry and begs Isaac to bless him as well. But it's too late. Jacob will indeed be the prosperous and honored brother.

Immediately, resentment, unforgiveness, and finally murderous rage fill Esau's heart. He says aloud to himself, *"The days of mourning for my father are near; then I will kill my brother Jacob"* (Genesis 27:41).

But Rebekah discovers Esau's intentions and tells Jacob to flee to her brother's home. Twenty years pass, and then Jacob makes a reconciliatory move toward Esau. He sends him a message about all he has acquired over the years and asks to find favor in his eyes. Esau responds. He is headed straight toward Jacob with 400 men. Jacob is terrified and divides his family and servants into two groups, hoping at least one group will be spared. He then prays for divine protection and gathers a slew of animals to go before him as pacifying gifts for Esau.

When Esau finally approaches, Jacob pays him homage fit for a king, bowing to the ground seven times. No sooner has he straightened back up when Esau runs to Jacob, embracing him and kissing him. The two men begin to weep, relishing in the peace, joy, and emotional relief that accompany reconciliation.

Jacob has these grateful words concerning a relationship restored:

> **"To see your face is like seeing the face of God, now that you have received me favorably."**
> **(Genesis 33:10)**

Ultimately the root of unresolved conflict springs from the inability to give or receive forgiveness. Only when a wounded heart offers forgiveness and an offender acknowledges and accepts forgiveness for the pain they have caused is reconciliation and a restored relationship possible.

You are not responsible for another's response to your efforts at reconciliation, but you are called to reflect the love of Christ by seeking forgiveness when you have caused harm and also by extending forgiveness just as God has forgiven you. This means that you are to forgive even when the offending person will not forgive you or acknowledge any wrongdoing, and you are to take the initiative to accept responsibility for your own faults.

▶ WRONG BELIEF:

"I have been so hurt and offended that I have no desire for reconciliation. Forgiveness is impossible because my offender will never change."

▶ RIGHT BELIEF:

"God offered reconciliation to me before I ever changed. Because Christ forgave me, I can seek restoration in my broken relationships by yielding my rights and allowing Christ to forgive through me."

"Bear with each other and forgive whatever grievances you may have against one another. Forgive as the Lord forgave you" (Colossians 3:13).

Plan of Salvation

Four Points of God's Plan

#1 God's Purpose for You is *Salvation*.

What was God's motivation in sending Jesus Christ to earth?

To express His love for you by saving you!

The Bible says ...

"God so loved the world that he gave his one and only Son, that whoever believes in him shall not perish but have eternal life. For God did not send his Son into the world to condemn the world, but to save the world through him" (John 3:16–17).

What was Jesus' purpose in coming to earth?

To forgive your sins, to empower you to have victory over sin, and to enable you to live a fulfilled life!

Jesus said ...

"I have come that they may have life, and that they may have it more abundantly" (John 10:10 NKJV).

#2 Your Problem is *Sin.*

What exactly is sin?

Sin is living independently of God's standard—knowing what is right, but choosing what is wrong.

The Bible says ...

"Anyone, then, who knows the good he ought to do and doesn't do it, sins" (James 4:17).

What is the major consequence of sin?

Spiritual death, eternal separation from God.

Scripture states ...

"Your iniquities [sins] *have separated you from your God"* (Isaiah 59:2).

"The wages of sin is death, but the gift of God is eternal life in Christ Jesus our Lord" (Romans 6:23).

#3 God's Provision for You is the *Savior.*

Can anything remove the penalty for sin?

Yes! Jesus died on the cross to personally pay the penalty for your sins.

The Bible says ...

"God demonstrates his own love for us in this: While we were still sinners, Christ died for us" (Romans 5:8).

What is the solution to being separated from God?

Belief in (entrusting your life to) Jesus Christ as the only way to God the Father.

Jesus says ...

"I am the way and the truth and the life. No one comes to the Father except through me" (John 14:6).

"Believe in the Lord Jesus, and you will be saved" (Acts 16:31).

#4 Your Part is *Surrender.*

Give Christ control of your life, entrusting yourself to Him.

"Jesus said to his disciples, 'If anyone would come after me, he must deny himself and take up his cross [die to your own self-rule] *and follow me. For whoever wants to save his life will lose it, but whoever loses his life for me will find it. What good will it be for a man if he gains the whole world, yet forfeits his soul?'"* (Matthew 16:24–26).

Place your faith in (rely on) Jesus Christ as your personal Lord and Savior and reject your "good works" as a means of earning God's approval.

"It is by grace you have been saved, through faith—and this not from yourselves, it is the gift of God—not by works, so that no one can boast" (Ephesians 2:8–9).

The moment you choose to receive Jesus as your Lord and Savior—entrusting your life to Him—He comes to live inside you. Then He gives you His power to live the fulfilled life God has planned for you. If you want to be fully forgiven by God and become the person God created you to be, you can tell Him in a simple, heartfelt prayer like this:

PRAYER OF SALVATION

"God, I want a real relationship with You.
I admit that many times I've chosen
to go my own way instead of Your way.
Please forgive me for my sins.
Jesus, thank You for dying on the cross
to pay the penalty for my sins.
Come into my life to be
my Lord and my Savior.
Change me from the inside out
and make me the person
You created me to be.
In Your holy name I pray. Amen."

WHAT CAN YOU NOW EXPECT?

If you sincerely prayed this prayer, look at what God says!

"Since we have been justified through faith, we have peace with God through our Lord Jesus Christ, through whom we have gained access by faith into this grace in which we now stand. And we rejoice in the hope of the glory of God."
(Romans 5:1–2)

STEPS TO SOLUTION

In Joseph's family, all of his brothers have the same color eyes: green. Green with envy because Joseph is their father's favorite son, endeared to Jacob because he was born to him in old age.

Furthermore, Jacob adorns Joseph in a richly ornamented robe while his other eleven sons are dressed in "ordinary" clothes.

Envy and resentment evolve into hate that is further intensified when Joseph shares with his brothers the two dreams he had.

The first dream:

**"We were binding sheaves of grain
out in the field when suddenly my sheaf
rose and stood upright,
while your sheaves gathered
around mine and bowed down to it."
(Genesis 37:7)**

The brothers are astounded and angered, replying:

**"Do you intend to reign over us?
Will you actually rule us?"
(Genesis 37:8)**

The second dream involves Joseph's entire family, and he shares it with his father as well. *"I had another dream, and this time the sun and moon and eleven stars were bowing down to me"* (Genesis 37:9).

Favorite son Joseph even manages to rile Jacob, who rebukes him for the dream's pompous pretense. And yet Jacob *"kept the matter in mind"* (Genesis 37:11).

Joseph's brothers, on the other hand, have murder in mind:

**"'Here comes that dreamer!'
they said to each other.
'Come now, let's kill him and throw him
into one of these cisterns and say
that a ferocious animal devoured him.
Then we'll see what comes of his dreams'"
(Genesis 37:19–20).**

Key Verse to Memorize

A voice of reason comes from Joseph's oldest brother, Reuben, who suggests they throw Joseph into a cistern instead of killing him—because he plans to secretly rescue his despised brother and return him to Jacob.

Joseph is placed in a cistern temporarily (with Reuben's knowledge), but ultimately the brothers decide (without Reuben's knowledge) to sell Joseph to trade merchants for 20 shekels of silver.

Reuben is panicked and grieved when he discovers what has happened, and immediately the cover-up begins. The brothers slaughter a goat and dip Joseph's treasured robe in it to deceive Jacob into thinking an animal has killed his beloved son. Overcome with pain and grief, Jacob mourns his "loss" for a long time.

One of the greatest challenges when treated cruelly is to live out the words of this Bible verse:

> *"Do not repay evil with evil or insult*
> *with insult, but with blessing,*
> *because to this you were called*
> *so that you may inherit a blessing."*
> (1 Peter 3:9)

Key Passages to Read

Carted off to Egypt as a slave, Joseph is sold in a divinely orchestrated exchange.

He isn't sold to an ordinary Egyptian citizen. Joseph finds himself becoming the property of Potiphar, the captain of the guard for Pharaoh. Because the Lord is with Joseph and gives him success in everything he does, Potiphar takes note and quickly promotes Joseph from slave to personal attendant.

Joseph becomes responsible for Potiphar's entire household and manager of all his affairs. Within a short time, blessing upon blessing abounds. *"From the time he put him in charge of his household and of all that he owned, the LORD blessed the household of the Egyptian because of Joseph"* (Genesis 39:5). Everything is going so right, but soon all goes so wrong.

"Now Joseph was well-built and handsome, and after a while his master's wife took notice of Joseph and said, 'Come to bed with me!'" (Genesis 39:6–7).

CHRIST'S CALL TO CHRISTIANS TO INITIATE RECONCILIATION:

▶ When you have wronged another ...

"If you are offering your gift at the altar and there remember that your brother has something against you, leave your gift there in front of the altar. First go and be reconciled to your brother; then come and offer your gift" (Matthew 5:23–24).

▶ When you have been wronged ...

"If your brother sins against you, go and show him his fault, just between the two of you. If he listens to you, you have won your brother over. But if he will not listen, take one or two others along, so that 'every matter may be established by the testimony of two or three witnesses.' If he refuses to listen to them, tell it to the church; and if he refuses to listen even to the church, treat him as you would a pagan or a tax collector. I tell you the truth, whatever you bind on earth will be bound in heaven, and whatever you loose on earth will be loosed in heaven" (Matthew 18:15–18).

The "Rs" of the Prodigal Son[23]

▶ **Request**

"Give me my share of the estate." (v. 12)

▶ **Rebellion**

"[He] squandered his wealth in wild living." (v. 13)

▶ **Repercussion**

"And he began to be in need." (v. 14)

▶ **Rejection**

"No one gave him anything." (v. 16)

▶ **Realization**

He came to his senses." (v. 17)

▶ **Resolution**

"I will ... go back to my father." (v. 18)

▶ **Repentance**

"I have sinned against heaven and against you." (v. 21)

▶ **Reconciliation**

"Bring the best robe and put it on him." (v. 22)

▶ **Redemption**

"Bring the fattened calf." (v. 23)

▶ **Rejoicing**

"This son of mine was dead and is alive ... they began to celebrate." (v. 24)

Why is this happening?

Joseph is a faithful servant to Potiphar, and an obedient servant to God. Day after day he refuses the sexual advances of Potiphar's wife, but ultimately she is a woman who won't take *no* for an answer.

Joseph arrives at Potiphar's home to attend to his duties and, oddly enough, no other servants can be found. The seductress grabs Joseph's cloak and once again seeks to snare him in her sexual net—*"Come to bed with me!"* (Genesis 39:12). Joseph flees, trying to get away from her as fast as possible. The scorned woman, rebuffed again, is now set on revenge.

Obviously, standing for what is right comes at a great price. With Joseph's cloak in hand, she calls for her household servants and lies to conceal her contempt. *"This Hebrew has been brought to us to make sport of us! He came in here to sleep with me, but I screamed. When he heard me scream for help, he left his cloak beside me and ran out of the house"* (Genesis 39:14–15).

But in truth, Joseph had posed a key question to his master's wife—a convicting question that she didn't want to hear: *"My master has withheld nothing from me except you, because you are his wife. How then could I do such a wicked thing and sin against God?"* (Genesis 39:9).

A Stubborn Heart

QUESTION: "What do I do if I can't persuade someone with a stubborn heart to reconcile?"

ANSWER: You are not responsible for the response of another person, but you are accountable to God to seek reconciliation. Each person is directly accountable before God.

> "Each of us will give
> an account of himself to God."
> (Romans 14:12)

Unresolved Anger

QUESTION: "Should I seek reconciliation even when I am still angry?"

ANSWER: Reconciliation will not take place if you have not dealt with your unresolved anger. Allow the Spirit of God to bring about true repentance on your part and an attitude that can soften the heart of the one offended.

> "An offended brother is more unyielding
> than a fortified city, and disputes
> are like the barred gates of a citadel."
> (Proverbs 18:19)

An Impossible Dream

QUESTION: "How do I know if I am only chasing an impossible dream by hoping for reconciliation in the future?"

ANSWER: You cannot know whether a broken relationship will truly be reconciled. No one but God has total knowledge of the future, and the Bible tells us that *"nothing is impossible with God"* (Luke 1:37). But if you respond to the Lord and to the conflict in a Christlike manner, you can assuredly have God's peace for the future.

> "Peace I leave with you; my peace I give you. I do not give to you as the world gives. Do not let your hearts be troubled and do not be afraid."
> (John 14:27)

Reconciliation Effort Fails

QUESTION: "What do I do if my effort to bring about reconciliation with someone fails?"

ANSWER: Others will be watching your response, so continue doing what is right.

> "We are taking pains to do what is right, not only in the eyes of the Lord but also in the eyes of men."
> (2 Corinthians 8:21)

Seek Forgiveness

QUESTION: "I was wrong in the way I related to a member of my family. What do I do if I think my sin is unforgiveable?"

ANSWER: You cannot know that you will not be forgiven. What you do know is that you are to go and ask forgiveness, making any necessary restitution, and leave the response of the other person to God. If forgiveness is extended, give thanks. If not, that person will have to give an account to God. Jesus said ...

"If you are offering your gift at the altar and there remember that your brother has something against you, leave your gift there in front of the altar. First go and be reconciled to your brother; then come and offer your gift."
(Matthew 5:23–24)

A Broken Relationship

QUESTION: "I've grieved over a broken relationship. Nothing I have done has moved us closer toward reconciliation. What can I do now?"

ANSWER: While a lack of restoration may be inevitable, a lack of forgiveness is not an option. Forgiveness is always required of us, no matter the circumstances.

> "Be kind and compassionate
> to one another, forgiving each other,
> just as in Christ God forgave you."
> (Ephesians 4:32)

Remarriage and Reconciliation

QUESTION: "When my mate left me and the children and married someone else, that ended all hope of remarriage for us. Isn't it wrong to hope for reconciliation?"

ANSWER: All relationships cannot be restored, but through the life-changing power of Christ, all people can be reconciled. When a marriage is dissolved by both divorce and remarriage, the original relationship cannot be restored. But it is possible for two divorced people to be reconciled to one another and to form a new, healthy, amicable relationship based on mutual respect, especially for the sake of children.

> "Do not repay anyone evil for evil.
> Be careful to do what is right
> in the eyes of everybody."
> (Romans 12:17)

Hostile Siblings

QUESTION: "How should I deal with my three siblings? Since our parents died, there has been so much hostility between us that we haven't spoken for years."

ANSWER: You might write each one a note stating that it would please and honor your parents if the four of you were in relationship again. Mention a positive character trait about each person. Let them all know that they are important to you. Ask if they would be open to starting a fresh, new relationship.

"One thing I do:
Forgetting what is behind
and straining toward what is ahead."
(Philippians 3:13)

▶ **Target #1:** *God's purpose* for me is to be a conformed to the character of Christ.

"For those God foreknew he also predestined to be conformed to the likeness of his Son, that he might be the firstborn among many brothers" (Romans 8:29).

- I'll do whatever it takes to be conformed to the character of Christ.

- I will be faithful to share the Good News—the Gospel—that we can be reconciled to God through the death of Jesus on the cross and His resurrection for the forgiveness of sins.

- Yielding to the transforming work of the Holy Spirit in my life will enable me to be a Christlike messenger of reconciliation.

- I am called to be a messenger of reconciliation, but I am not responsible for how people respond.

"We are therefore Christ's ambassadors, as though God were making his appeal through us." (2 Corinthians 5:20)

▶**Target #2:** *God's priority* for me is to line up my thinking with God's thinking.

"Do not conform any longer to the pattern of this world, but be transformed by the renewing of your mind. Then you will be able to test and approve what God's will is—his good, pleasing and perfect will" (Romans 12:2).

- I'll do whatever it takes to line up my thinking with God's thinking.

- I will do everything I can to reconcile my broken relationships.

- I recognize that all relationships will not be restored, but reconciliation is still possible.

- I know that the Lord is pleased when I strive for peace and harmony.

> **"How good and pleasant it is when brothers live together in unity!"**
> **(Psalm 133:1)**

▶ **Target #3:** *God's plan* is to help me as I seek to obey Him by reconciling.

"Yes, and I ask you, loyal yokefellow, help these women who have contended at my side in the cause of the gospel, along with Clement and the rest of my fellow workers, whose names are in the book of life" (Philippians 4:3).

- I'll do whatever it takes to rely on Christ's strength, not on my strength.

- With God's empowering, reconciliation is possible.

- Before attempting to reconcile, I will seek God's counsel and His strength through prayer.

- I will rely on God to help me develop healthy relationships.

> **"It is God who works in you to will and to act according to his good purpose."**
> **(Philippians 2:13)**

Joseph is thrown into prison for the alleged rape, but instead of hardening his heart, he surrenders his heart to God. Therefore, as previously with Potiphar, God grants Joseph favor with the warden, and in no time he is put in charge of all of the prison's administrative affairs. Even in prison, *"the Lord was with him; he showed him kindness"* (Genesis 39:21).

One day, Joseph is assigned to oversee two special prisoners, Pharaoh's chief cupbearer and his chief baker. Somehow they had enraged the Supreme Ruler of Egypt and were imprisoned.

Eventually, each has a dream on the same night, which Joseph interprets with divine insight. In three days the cupbearer will be restored to Pharaoh's favor, but in three days the baker will be hanged! Joseph asks the cupbearer to mention him to Pharaoh when he is restored to his former position.

But the cupbearer forgets all about Joseph, and two full years pass.

The Bible instructs ...

> **"Wait for the Lord; be strong
> and take heart and wait for the Lord."
> (Psalm 27:14)**

THE HEART TEST

▶Do my actions **demonstrate love** toward my offender?

"Love your enemies" (Matthew 5:44).

▶Do I **speak well** of my offender?

"Bless those who curse you, pray for those who mistreat you" (Luke 6:28).

▶Do I do **what is right** toward my offender?

"Do not repay anyone evil for evil. Be careful to do what is right in the eyes of everybody" (Romans 12:17).

▶Do I have a **forgiving spirit** toward my offender?

"If you forgive men when they sin against you, your heavenly Father will also forgive you. But if you do not forgive men their sins, your Father will not forgive your sins" (Matthew 6:14–15).

▶Do I exhibit **meekness** toward my offender?

"Blessed are the meek, for they will inherit the earth" (Matthew 5:5).

▶Do I show **deference** toward my offender?

"Do nothing out of selfish ambition or vain conceit, but in humility consider others better than yourselves" (Philippians 2:3).

▶ Do I **pray** on behalf of my offender?

"Pray for those who persecute you"
(Matthew 5:44).

▶ Do I focus on **eternal values** when I think of my offender?

"You have been raised with Christ, set your hearts on things above, where Christ is seated at the right hand of God. Set your minds on things above, not on earthly things. For you died, and your life is now hidden with Christ in God" (Colossians 3:1–3).

In your heart, have you ever said to yourself, "I would be willing to forgive if he would admit he was wrong, or I would let go of the past if she would just say she's sorry." Conditional acceptance is an attitude of the heart. The heart communicates acceptance or rejection.

Joseph finds himself on the road to reconciliation and it all begins with the correct interpretation of two more dreams. But these are Pharaoh's dreams.

The ruler of Egypt becomes frustrated because none of his wise officials can interpret two troubling dreams. The chief cupbearer's mind drifts back to the dungeon. Suddenly he remembers Joseph and describes his experiences to Pharaoh. Immediately Pharaoh summons Joseph, who humbly conveys, *"I cannot do it ... but God will give Pharaoh the answer he desires"* (Genesis 41:16).

Indeed Pharaoh receives a startling interpretation: Egypt will experience abundance followed by seven years of famine. Additionally, Joseph gave wise counsel about how to prepare for the next 14 years. Ultimately Joseph's discernment is unmatched in Pharaoh's eyes, so he proceeds to honor him as second-in-command over Egypt.

Imagine, from the dank dungeon to royal residence—all in God's perfect timing. But Joseph had to *wait* to be led by the Lord—and *wait* to understand the perfect will of the Lord.

"A man's steps are directed by the LORD. How then can anyone understand his own way?" (Proverbs 20:24)

To sue or not to sue—that is the question! When you have been wronged, what is the right way to proceed? The major Scripture passage dealing with civil suits is 1 Corinthians 6:1–7. This passage encourages God's people to settle their problems outside of court. Disputes between Christians should be addressed between the individuals themselves or with the help of other Christians. (Read Matthew 18:15–17.) Civil action with an unbeliever is not forbidden, but God's heart on courtroom litigation is seen in this Bible verse:

"As you are going with your adversary to the magistrate, try hard to be reconciled to him on the way, or he may drag you off to the judge, and the judge turn you over to the officer, and the officer throw you into prison."
(Luke 12:58)

71

If it is your heart's desire to have a ministry of reconciliation, avoiding civil suits will produce the following six results and will bring honor to God as you reflect a life that lives in accordance with His Word:

▶ **Prevents** taking your argument to a public court (Luke 12:58).

▶ **Encourages** a biblical solution (1 Corinthians 6:1–7).

▶ **Reflects** an example of our reconciliation to God through Christ (Romans 5:10).

▶ **Demonstrates** sacrificial love (Matthew 5:44).

▶ **Highlights** our testimony as obedient to the Word of God (Matthew 5:38–41).

▶ **Improves** our ability to help others move toward reconciliation (2 Corinthians 5:18–20).

"Fools mock at making amends for sin, but goodwill is found among the upright." (Proverbs 14:9)

Remember the sheaves, and the sun, moon, and stars?

The seven years of abundance are a faint memory. Famine has now swept across Egypt, and Joseph is in charge of selling the grain that has been stored. Famine even encompasses Canaan, where Jacob and his eleven sons live. Jacob sends them all except Benjamin, brother to Joseph and the only other child birthed by his beloved Rachel, to Egypt to buy grain.

When the brothers see the Egyptian royal official who is selling grain, they bow down, faces all the way to the ground. They do not recognize Joseph, but Joseph immediately recognizes them. He speaks harshly to them and accuses them of being spies, but he pries by inquiring about their family, their father, and the brother left at home. They eventually return home with grain, but Joseph warns them that they'll never see his face again unless they bring Benjamin.

Eventually, Jacob and his sons need to purchase more grain, and the reluctant father acquiesces and allows Benjamin to accompany his brothers to Egypt, where the hatchet will finally be buried.

And that hatchet, according to Scripture, should never, ever surface again.

> **"Peter came to Jesus and asked,
> 'Lord, how many times shall I forgive my
> brother when he sins against me?
> Up to seven times?'
> Jesus answered, 'I tell you, not seven
> times, but seventy-seven times.'"**
> **(Matthew 18:21–22)**

The tomahawk, or war hatchet, once a weapon of Native Americans, bears a distinctive history. Used as war clubs and hunting weapons, the original tomahawks had heads made of flint or bronze tied to wooden handles with cords of animal skin. The ceremonial tomahawk, decorated with brightly colored feathers or porcupine-quill work, used to be buried when peace was made with an enemy and dug up when peace was broken.

From this old Native American custom comes the expression "bury the hatchet," a phrase that means "a sincere commitment to forgive and be reconciled!"[24] Unfortunately, many people today bury the hatchet but intentionally leave the handle exposed! Instead, they want to ready themselves to pay back wrong for wrong—if they feel justified.

> **"Make sure that nobody pays back wrong
> for wrong, but always try to be kind to
> each other and to everyone else."**
> **(1 Thessalonians 5:15)**

▶ **Prepare your heart** for seeking reconciliation.

- Be willing to view the conflict as an opportunity for growth.[25]

- Be willing to learn what God wants you to learn.[26]

- Be willing to discover that you are partly at fault.[27]

- Be willing to expose your weaknesses.

- Be willing to be open with your feelings.

- Be willing to accept a negative outcome and move on in forgiveness.

- Be willing to pray for God's will to be done.

"Let the peace of Christ rule in your hearts, since as members of one body you were called to peace. And be thankful" (Colossians 3:15).

▶ **Know that refusal** to seek reconciliation affects the intimacy of your fellowship with God.

Humble your heart and pray:

- "Lord, I don't want to be proud and unbending."

- "Lord, I want Your favor on my life, not Your disfavor."

- "Lord, I want to reflect Your character and be open to reconciliation."

"If you are offering your gift at the altar and there remember that your brother has something against you, leave your gift there in front of the altar. First go and be reconciled to your brother; then come and offer your gift" (Matthew 5:23–24).

▶ **Seek forgiveness and apologize** for words that have hurt the other person, be conciliatory.

- "I have tried to see our relationship from your point of view."

- "I realize that I've been wrong in my attitude of _____."

- "Would you be willing to forgive me?"

"If you have been trapped by what you said, ensnared by the words of your mouth, then do this, my son, to free yourself, since you have fallen into your neighbor's hands: Go and humble yourself; press your plea with your neighbor!" (Proverbs 6:2–3).

▶ **Recognize the ground rules** of communication.[28]

- Offer unconditional acceptance.

- Confront the problem, not the person.

- Listen without interrupting.

- Verbalize feelings.

- Use words that build self-worth.

- Aim for mutual understanding.

- Give more than you take.

"Be completely humble and gentle; be patient, bearing with one another in love" (Ephesians 4:2).

▶**Be kind and gentle**, trusting God to work in the heart of the other person.[29]

- Don't harbor resentment.

- Don't make excuses for yourself.

- Don't get drawn into arguments.

- Don't fail to pray.

- Don't have expectations of immediate acceptance.

"The Lord's servant must not quarrel; instead, he must be kind to everyone, able to teach, not resentful. Those who oppose him he must gently instruct, in the hope that God will grant them repentance leading them to a knowledge of the truth" (2 Timothy 2:24–25).

▶**Reflect the character of Christ** in all that you do.

In order to prepare your heart to reflect the character of Christ, pray:

- "Lord, I die to my personal rights."

   "I have been crucified with Christ and I no

longer live, but Christ lives in me. The life I live in the body, I live by faith in the Son of God, who loved me and gave himself for me" (Galatians 2:20).

- "Lord, I die to having to defend myself."

   "The LORD is my strength and my shield; my heart trusts in him, and I am helped" (Psalm 28:7).

- "Lord, I die to relying on my own abilities."

   "He who trusts in himself is a fool, but he who walks in wisdom is kept safe" (Proverbs 28:26).

▶ **Enlist a mediator** if necessary.[30]

- Pray for God to prepare the heart of your offender for mediation.

- Seek a person whom your offender can respect.

- Say, "An outside person can have a different perspective that is objective. Would you be willing to consider a mediator to help us think through our problems with the hope of achieving reconciliation?"

"If he will not listen [to you], *take one or two others along, so that 'every matter may be established by the testimony of two or three witnesses'"* (Matthew 18:16).

▶ **Do not hold yourself responsible** for the outcome.[31]

- You cannot force reconciliation to occur.

- When reconciliation is refused, don't live with false guilt.

- A lack of reconciliation will not be wasted—God will bring something good out of it.

"We know that in all things God works for the good of those who love him, who have been called according to his purpose" (Romans 8:28).

▶ **Rest in the knowledge** that you have done all you can do to seek peace.

- Continue to show love, and treat the other person with forgiveness.

- Thank God for giving you the desire to be at peace with everyone.

- Praise God for His commitment to orchestrate your own spiritual growth.

"If it is possible, as far as it depends on you, live at peace with everyone" (Romans 12:18).

There are no guarantees that any relationship will be reconciled, so when your attempts to reconcile are rejected, remember ...[32]

▶ **If your heart has been repentant**, you have God's total forgiveness.

"If we claim to be without sin, we deceive ourselves and the truth is not in us. If we confess our sins, he is faithful and just and will forgive us our sins and purify us from all unrighteousness" (1 John 1:8–9).

▶ **Pray for the one who refuses reconciliation**—there is an unmet need.

"Love your enemies and pray for those who persecute you" (Matthew 5:44).

▶ **God never leaves you** when you suffer the loss of a close relationship.

"The LORD is close to the brokenhearted and saves those who are crushed in spirit" (Psalm 34:18).

▶ **Control what you say** about those who refuse reconciliation.

"Bless those who persecute you; bless and do not curse" (Romans 12:14).

▶ **Don't be vengeful**—in time, God will deal with those who do wrong.

"Do not take revenge, my friends, but leave room for God's wrath, for it is written: 'It is mine to avenge; I will repay,' says the Lord" (Romans 12:19).

▶ **God will do a work in you** that is good in spite of the difficulty.

"And we know that in all things God works for the good of those who love him, who have been called according to his purpose" (Roman 8:28).

When Reconciliation Does Happen

After observing Joseph's initial behavior toward his brothers, it appears reconciliation is refused, but his heart melts when he lays eyes on Benjamin.

"Deeply moved at the sight of his brother, Joseph hurried out and looked for a place to weep. He went into his private room and wept there" (Genesis 43:30).

Joseph had invited his brothers to his home for a meal, and when they initially see him they *bow low* to honor him. Following the meal Joseph can no longer control himself; he dismisses his servants and is left standing alone before his brothers. *"He wept so loudly that the Egyptians heard him, and Pharaoh's household heard about it"* (Genesis 45:2).

Finally Joseph regains enough composure to blurt out, *"I am Joseph!"* (Genesis 45:3). He inquires about his father, if he is still living, and the eleven brothers stand before him speechless and terrified.

Joseph then takes a giant step toward reconciliation with his brothers by saying, *"And now, do not be distressed and do not be angry with yourselves for selling me here, because it was to save lives that God sent me ahead of you. For two years now there has been famine in the land, and for the next five years there will not be plowing and reaping. But God sent me ahead of you to preserve for you a remnant on earth and to save your lives by a great deliverance. So then, it was not you who sent me here, but God. He made me father to Pharaoh, lord of his entire household and ruler of all Egypt"* (Genesis 45:5–8).

And later he stated with undeniable strength ...

"You intended to harm me,
but God intended it for good to
accomplish what is now being done,
the saving of many lives."
(Genesis 50:20)

> *Reconciliation is a restored*
> *relationship based on restored trust.*
> *It requires repentance and is to be*
> *extended only when earned.*
> *—June Hunt*

SCRIPTURES TO MEMORIZE

You can choose to have a **ministry of reconciliation**.

> *"If anyone is in Christ, he is a new creation; the old has gone, the new has come! All this is from God, who reconciled us to himself through Christ and gave us the **ministry of reconciliation**."* (2 Corinthians 5:17–18)

You can **do what is right** and be at **peace**.

> *"Do not repay anyone evil for evil. Be careful to **do what is right** in the eyes of everybody. If it is possible, as far as it depends on you, live at **peace** with everyone."* (Romans 12:17–18)

You can **humble yourself** when your **words** have been unwise.

> *"If you have been trapped by what you said, ensnared by the **words** of your mouth, then do this, my son, to free yourself, since you have fallen into your neighbor's hands: Go and **humble yourself**; press your plea with your neighbor!"* (Proverbs 6:2–3)

You can ask forgiveness of someone who **has something against you.**

> *"If you are offering your gift at the altar and there remember that your brother **has something against you**, leave your gift there in front of the altar. First go and be reconciled to your brother; then come and offer your gift."* (Matthew 5:23–24)

You can choose to confront when someone **sins against you**.

> *"If your brother **sins against you**, go and show him his fault, just between the two of you. If he listens to you, you have won your brother over. But if he will not listen, take one or two others along, so that 'every matter may be established by the testimony of two or three witnesses.'"* (Matthew 18:15–16)

You can choose to **forgive** someone who **sins against you**.

> *"If you **forgive** men when they **sin against you**, your heavenly Father will also forgive you. But if you do not forgive men their sins, your Father will not forgive your sins."* (Matthew 6:14–15)

You can choose to pray **for those who persecute you.**

> *"Love your enemies and **pray for those who persecute you**."* (Matthew 5:44)

You can **build others up** even if they have hurt you.

> "Do not let any unwholesome talk come out of your mouths, but only what is helpful for **building others up** according to their needs, that it may benefit those who listen." (Ephesians 4:29)

You can make a choice not to **harden** your **heart**.

> "Blessed is the man who always fears the LORD, but he who **hardens** his **heart** falls into trouble." (Proverbs 28:14)

You can make a choice to **overcome evil with good**.

> "'If your enemy is hungry, feed him; if he is thirsty, give him something to drink. In doing this, you will heap burning coals on his head.' Do not be overcome by evil, but **overcome evil with good**." (Romans 12:20-21)

NOTES

1. James Strong, *The Exhaustive Concordance of the Bible: Showing Every Word of the Text of the Common English Version of the Canonical Books, and Every Occurrence of Each Word in Regular Order*, electronic ed. (Ontario: Woodside Bible Fellowship, 1996) #H3722.

2. Strong, *The Exhaustive Concordance of the Bible*, #G2644.

3. Gary McSpadden, "He Paid a Debt" *Actors Speak Louder Than Words & 1,020 Other Titles* (n.p.: Magnolia Hill Music, 2000).

4. *Merriam-Webster's Dictionary of Basic English*, s.v. "Reconcile;" s.v. "Reconciliation."

5. *Merriam-Webster*, s.v. "Alienation."

6. Robert Laird Harris, Gleason Leonard Archer, Bruce K. Waltke, *Theological Wordbook of the Old Testament*, electronic ed. (Chicago: Moody Press, 1999), # 843.

7. Strong, *The Exhaustive Concordance of the Bible*, #H2114.

8. Strong, *The Exhaustive Concordance of the Bible*, #G526.

9. *Merriam-Webster*, s.v. "Alienate."

10. *Merriam-Webster*, s.v. "Mediation."

11. L. Randolph Lowry and Richard W. Meyers, *Conflict Management and Counseling, Resources for Christian Counseling*, ed. Gary R. Collins, vol. 29 (Waco, TX: Word, 1991), 107.

12. Strong, *The Exhaustive Concordance of the Bible*, #H3887.

13. Strong, *The Exhaustive Concordance of the Bible*, #G3316.

14. Ken Sande, *The Peacemaker: A Biblical Guide to Resolving Personal Conflict* (Grand Rapids: Baker, 1991), 145.

15. Sande, *Peacemaker*, 145, 147.

16. *American Heritage Science Dictionary* (New York: Houghton Mifflin, 2005), s.v. "Mediate."

17. Lynn Buzzard, Juanita Buzzard, and Laury Eck, *Readiness for Reconciliation: A Biblical Guide* (Oak Park, IL: Christian Conciliation Service, 1982), 7; James Pittman, *What Do You Do with a Broken Relationship?* (Grand Rapids, MI: Radio Bible Class, 2002), 2–3.

18. Pittman, *What Do You Do with a Broken Relationship?* 6–7, 12–13.

19. Don Baker, *Restoring Broken Relationships* (Eugene, OR: Harvest House, 1989), 88–89.

20. Pittman, *What Do You Do with a Broken Relationship?* 8, 18–20.

21. Pittman, *What Do You Do with a Broken Relationship?* 11.

22. Lawrence J. Crabb, Jr., *Understanding People: Deep Longings for Relationship*, Ministry Resources Library (Grand Rapids: Zondervan, 1987), 15–16; Robert S. McGee, *The Search for Significance*, 2nd ed. (Houston, TX: Rapha, 1990), 27–30.

23. Stuart Briscoe, *Living Dangerously* (Grand Rapids: Zondervan, 1968), 59.

24. Francis Jennings, William Fenton, Mary Druke, and David Miller, *The History and Culture of Iroquois Diplomacy: An Interdisciplinary Guide to the Treaties of the Six Nations and Their League* (Syracuse, NY: Syracuse University Press, 1985), 118.

25. Myron Rush, *Hope for Hurting Relationships* (Wheaton, IL: Victor, 1989), 119–120.

26. Sande, *Peacemaker*, 21–25.

27. Sande, *Peacemaker*, 93–109.

28. Rush, *Hope for Hurting Relationships*, 123.

29. Pittman, *What Do You Do with a Broken Relationship?* 23.

30. Pittman, *What Do You Do with a Broken Relationship?* 23–24.

31. Pittman, *What Do You Do with a Broken Relationship?* 22.

32. Sande, *Peacemaker*, 197–204; Pittman, *What Do You Do with a Broken Relationship?* 22–26.

SELECTED BIBLIOGRAPHY

Allender, Dan B., and Tremper Longman III. *Bold Love: A Discussion Guide Based on the Book*. Colorado Springs, CO: NavPress, 1992.

Baker, Don. *Restoring Broken Relationships*. Eugene, OR: Harvest House, 1989.

Buzzard, Lynn, Juanita Buzzard, and Laury Eck. *Readiness for Reconciliation: A Biblical Guide*. Oak Park, IL: Christian Conciliation Service, 1982.

Dawson, John. *What Christians Should Know About Reconciliation*. Ventura, CA: International Reconciliation Coalition, 1998.

Hunt, June. *Counseling Through Your Bible Handbook*. Eugene, Oregon: Harvest House Publishers, 2008.

Hunt, June. *Hope for Your Heart: Finding Strength in Life's Storms*. Wheaton, ILL: Crossway Books, 2011.

Hunt, June. *How to Defeat Harmful Habits*. Eugene, OR: Harvest House, 2011.

Hunt, June. *How to Forgive ... When You Don't Feel Like It*. Eugene, Oregon: Harvest House Publishers, 2007.

Hunt, June. *How to Handle Your Emotions*. Eugene, Oregon: Harvest House Publishers, 2008.

Hunt, June. *How to Rise Above Abuse*. Eugene, OR: Harvest House, 2010.

Hunt, June. *Keeping Your Cool ... When Your Anger Is Hot!* Eugene, Oregon: Harvest House Publishers, 2009.

Hunt, June. *Seeing Yourself Through God's Eyes*. Eugene, OR: Harvest House, 2008.

Lowry, L. Randolph and Richard W. Meyers. *Conflict Management and Counseling*. Resources for Christian Counseling, ed. Gary R. Collins, vol. 29. Waco, TX: Word, 1991.

Lynch, Chuck. *"I Should Forgive, But ..." Finding Release from Anger and Bitterness*. Nashville: Word, 1998.

McGuire, Paul, and Kristina McGuire. *Heal Your Past and Change Your Marriage*. Lake Mary, FL: Creation House, 2000.

Moore, Michael S. *Reconciliation: A Study of Biblical Families in Conflict*. Joplin, MO: College Press, 1994.

Nygren, Bruce. *Touching the Shadows: A Love Tested and Renewed*. Nashville: Thomas Nelson, 2000.

Rebuilder's Guide. Oak Brook, Ill.: Institute in Basic Life Principles, 1982.

Rodgers, Beverly, and Tom Rodgers. *Soul-Healing Love: Ten Practical Easy-to-Learn Techniques for Couples in Crisis*. San Jose, CA: Resource, 1998.

Rush, Myron. *Hope for Hurting Relationships*. Wheaton, IL: Victor, 1989.

Sande, Ken. *The Peacemaker: A Biblical Guide to Resolving Personal Conflict*. Grand Rapids: Baker, 1991.

Tosini, Joseph. *She Called Me Dad: Hope for Relationship in a Wounded World*. Columbia, MO: Cityhill, 1990.

What Do You Do With a Broken Relationship? Radio Bible Class, [cited 28 August 2002]. http://www.gospelcom.net/rbc/ds/q0703/q0703.html.

White, John, and Ken Blue. *Church Discipline that Heals: Putting Costly Love into Action*. Downers Grove, IL: InterVarsity, 1985.

Williams, Pat, Jill Williams, and Jerry Jenkins. *Rekindled*. Old Tappan, NJ: Fleming H. Revell, 1985.

June Hunt's HOPE FOR THE HEART minibooks are biblically-based, and full of practical advice that is relevant, spiritually-fulfilling and wholesome.

HOPE FOR THE HEART TITLES

Adultery .... ISBN 9781596366848
Alcohol & Drug Abuse .... ISBN 9781596366596
Anger .... ISBN 9781596366411
Codependency .... ISBN 9781596366510
Conflict Resolution .... ISBN 9781596366473
Confrontation .... ISBN 9781596366886
Considering Marriage .... ISBN 9781596366763
Decision Making .... ISBN 9781596366534
Depression .... ISBN 9781596366497
Domestic Violence .... ISBN 9781596366824
Fear .... ISBN 9781596366701
Forgiveness .... ISBN 9781596366435
Friendship .... ISBN 9781596368828
Gambling .... ISBN 9781596366862
Grief .... ISBN 9781596366572
Guilt .... ISBN 9781596366961
Hope .... ISBN 9781596366558
Loneliness .... ISBN 9781596366909
Manipulation .... ISBN 9781596366749
Marriage .... ISBN 9781596368941
Parenting .... ISBN 9781596366725
Reconciliation .... ISBN 9781596368897
Rejection .... ISBN 9781596366787
Self-Worth .... ISBN 9781596366688
Sexual Integrity .... ISBN 9781596366947
Singleness .... ISBN 9781596368774
Stress .... ISBN 9781596368996
Success Through Failure .... ISBN 9781596366923
Suicide Prevention .... ISBN 9781596366800
Verbal & Emotional Abuse .... ISBN 9781596366459

www.aspirepress.com

The HOPE FOR THE HEART
Biblical Counseling Library
is Your Solution!

- Easy-to-read, perfect for anyone.
- Short. Only 96 pages. Good for the busy person.
- Christ-centered biblical advice and practical help
- Tested and proven over 20 years of June Hunt's radio ministry
- 30 titles in the series – each tackling a key issue people face today.
- Affordable. You or your church can give away, lend, or sell them.

Display available for churches and ministries.

www.aspirepress.com